The Best Baby Sleep Book

*The New Revolutionary Method to get your Baby to Sleep
Through the Night*

Edward Kulich M.D., F.A.A.P.

Foreword by Jill Zarin
Author of *Secrets of a Jewish Mother*, and star of
The Real Housewives of New York

Pediatric Press
A division of KidsHousecalls
1601 Voorhies Ave, 2nd Fl
Brooklyn, NY 11235

First Pediatric Press paperback edition April 2012

KidsHousecalls is a registered trademark of Edward Kulich M.D.

For information about speaking engagements or special discounts for bulk purchases, please contact KidsHousecalls@gmail.com or call 917-617-2194.

10 9 8 7 6 5 4 3 2 1

ISBN 978-0-9854494-1-4
ISBN 978-0-9854494-2-1(ebook)
ISBN 978-0-9854494-3-8 (audiobook)

To Jaclyn, Jason, and Bianca, and to George, without whom, none of this would have been possible.

DISCLAIMER:
This book contains advice of a general nature and may not be specific to your child's individual needs. Always consult a doctor regarding any health questions specific to your child.

Foreword

Dr. Kulich, one of Manhattan's top pediatricians, has filled a void with *The Best Baby Sleep Book*. Being a mother is one of the toughest jobs out there. Hectic schedules, dirty diapers, play-dates, and taking care of your family in general is a demanding task. When a baby or child doesn't sleep, it puts a strain on not just mom, but the whole family. A good night's sleep is essential for a family to function, and this book provides all the right tools for parents to take back control of their baby's schedule.

After bringing house calls back into the mainstream with KidsHousecalls, his revolutionary pediatric house call practice, he has changed sleep training by challenging the all too common one-size-fits-all approach to getting your baby to sleep through the night.

Unlike other pediatricians and sleep consultants, Dr. Kulich tailors his approach to each child, and explains things easily and thoughtfully. As a how-to guide, this book contains everything you need to know and is packed with straightforward methods that anyone can use to sleep train their babies. Dr. Kulich's pediatric practice and sleep training service has taken New York by storm, and many of Manhattan's elite depend on him not only for the finest care for their children, but to finally get that good night's sleep they deserve.

        -**Jill Zarin,** Star of *Real Housewives of New York* and author of *Secrets of a Jewish Mother.*

Introduction

If you are sitting down to read this book, odds are you have some kind of caffeinated beverage as your reading partner. You may be frustrated, tired, and short on time. Having a baby is one of the most amazing, life changing experiences one can have. As a father, a pediatrician, and an infant sleep consultant, I understand what you are going through. I've been there myself.

Being a parent is a tough job. Having a baby that does not sleep makes things hard on you, your baby, and your entire family. The last thing a sleep deprived parent needs is a dense, comprehensive infant sleep book. You need something that quickly identifies your child's sleep issues, and gives you an easy-to-follow road map to solve them.

Unlike every other infant sleep book out there, this book does not go into the science of infant sleep. I will not talk about REM and non-REM sleep. I will not go into topics that you don't care about. I will get to the point and address the task at hand: getting your baby to sleep through the night. This book is not a comprehensive reference, but a specific, proven approach to fix your little one's sleeping problems.

Prior to embarking on any sleep training, you must address medical issues that make your child uncomfortable, cranky, and detract from restful sleep. Unresolved medical issues are the achilles heel of sleep training, and no sleep training program will be effective for a baby who is crying because they are uncomfortable, or in pain.

This book provides a no-nonsense, streamlined approach to addressing and treating issues that prevent your baby from sleeping through the night. Often, more than one problem exists at the same time, and the approach needs to be organized, and carried out in a particular order. I invite you to read the medical chapters to see if your baby matches the descriptions presented here. If your baby does not match any of the described medical problems, you may then implement the behavioral techniques in the order they are presented.

This book is drawn upon my experiences as not only a pediatrician, but as a pediatric sleep consultant. My practice, www.BabySleepDoctor.com is exclusively dedicated to infants and children who have difficulty sleeping through the night.

So let's embark on an exciting journey to achieving better sleep for you and your baby.

Edward Kulich, M.D. F.A.A.P

1

Acid Reflux

The internet is littered with books and websites that promise to get your baby to sleep through the night in a set period of time. Quotes such as "Your baby will sleep through the night in 3 days or your money back" are commonplace. While a set of canned instructions may work for some, sleep issues in infants are usually more complicated and may be a result of more than one problem. I frequently encounter babies with sleep issues due to medical problems, and acid reflux is by far the most common.

Lets look at Baby Sean's story...

Sean's parents were at their wits end. Sean was a sweet baby who was gaining weight well. Mealtime and bedtime, however, were always a challenge. He was very fussy during his feeds. He would thrash around and pull away, but always seemed hungry. Sean would cry incessantly when he was placed in his crib for naps and for nighttime sleep. White noise machines, pacifiers, and every possible book and gimmick were tried without success. Everyone said that Sean was just a colicky baby and would grow out of it. Going with recommendations from family and friends, Sean's parents tried gas drops without effect. The only thing that seemed to work to get Sean to sleep would be either rocking him to sleep or driving him around. Frequently, Sean's parents would take a ride around the block until he fell asleep. They would then unsnap the car-seat and bring it in the house. When Sean's mother brought him to the pediatrician, she was told that it was colic and he would grow out of it.

What no one seemed to realize was that Sean had a very common medical condition that was interfering with his ability to sleep: acid reflux. Acid reflux is quite common and many people (Doctors included) tend to brush off subtle reflux symptoms if a child is gaining weight. Only severe cases of reflux result in failure to gain weight. Reflux is under-diagnosed, and without a doubt the most frequent medical cause of sleep problems in infants.

SYMPTOMS OF ACID REFLUX:

✓ Arching during feeds

✓ Stopping midway through feeds and becoming hungry relatively quickly, resulting in an infant that takes small meals frequently.

✓ Takes small volume feeds frequently

✓ Spits up frequently

✓ Lip smacking

✓ A funny face during or after feeding.

✓ Pulling away from the bottle

✓ Crankiness during or right after feeds

✓ Refusal to lie down (on a full or empty stomach)

✓ Constant congestion

Many cases of acid reflux get better by 4-6 months of age when solids are introduced, and the junction between the food-pipe (esophagus) and the stomach matures. Keep in mind that an occasional spit-up is not uncommon and does not mean your baby has reflux. However, reflux symptoms can be subtle and are frequently overlooked.

Here you see the stomach and food pipe (esophagus). This is a normal infant, where the stomach acid is not going up.

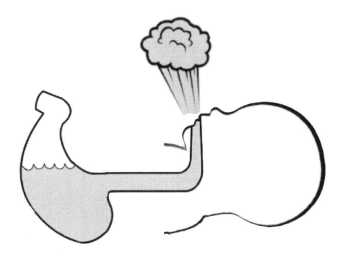

The picture above shows classic reflux. I call this "no-brainer reflux." In classic reflux, the stomach contents go up the foodpipe (esophagus) and out. Parents of babies with classic reflux do a lot of laundry because its not uncommon for the infant to spit up a significant percentage of each feed. Extreme cases of classic reflux even result in failure to gain weight because the child cannot keep down enough calories.

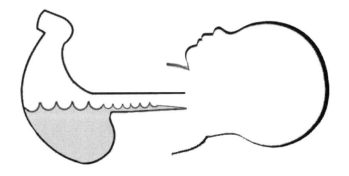

The above picture shows what I see most commonly in my practice, so called *"subtle reflux."* In the above picture, the stomach acid goes up into the foodpipe and but doesn't always manifest in the classic vomiting symptoms referred to in the previous example. This scenario is not bad enough to cause frequent spitting, or even spitting at all. The child does not thrash around during feeds, and gains weight, but if prompted with the right questions, this condition can be diagnosed and treated.

It is important to realize that since reflux is a medical problem that causes physical pain and discomfort, no amount of sleep training will get results until this is treated.

How is acid reflux treated?

Acid reflux is treated with non-medical interventions, and for more significant cases, medication. Treatment of reflux without using medication includes elevating the head of the crib with a wedge under the mattress, and by thickening the formula or breast-milk with rice cereal. If reflux is significant enough, medications that stop the production of stomach acid can be helpful (such as Ranitidine and Lansoprazole). If I suspect reflux, I will typically try a week or two of Ranitidine and watch for a response. Significant improvement in symptoms will usually help make the diagnosis. I typically hear one of two things from parents when I try acid blockers: "Thank you so much! I feel like I we were just issued a completely different baby! I wish we would have tried it sooner." or "There is no change."

If there is no benefit from acid blockers, the diagnosis of reflux is usually excluded, allowing us to look at other factors interfering with sleep.

If you think that your baby may have acid reflux, you should contact your pediatrician to discuss the possibility of reflux, and whether or not treatment is necessary.

How to thicken formula:

Many parents   will attempt to thicken the formula for their infant by scooping a teaspoon of rice cereal into the bottle of formula/breast milk. This is wrong. The point of thickening the formula is to make the consistency thick enough so that it is difficult for the formula to go back up. The correct way to thicken formula and breast milk is *one tablespoon of rice cereal per ounce of formula.*

A special nipple is required to allow the thicker mixture to flow through. The problem with putting so much cereal into the bottle is that you are not just thickening the formula, you are adding calories as well, which may lead to excessive weight gain. There are commercially available formulas that have increased consistency without the extra calories.

When Medical Issues Cause Behavioral Problems:

Lets look back at baby Sean:

Sean's reflux was identified and treated. His eating improved, he didn't thrash around anymore during feeds, and was a happier baby, but he still did not sleep through the night. Mom found that she had trouble putting him down in the crib because, although he didn't seem as fussy, he wanted to be held and to fall asleep in moms arms. In the middle of the night, Sean would still wake up for a feed.

What happened here?

This is a classic example of how a medical issue sets you up for a behavioral issue . The initial problem, the reflux, has been addressed, but after several months of being rocked to sleep and expecting a nighttime feed, a happier Sean was not going to let mom off the hook so easy! Sean wanted to be held as he fell asleep and was used to eating when he woke up in the middle of the night. Once I had Sean's reflux under control, we had to work on his routine and feeding problems.   First, we worked on his nighttime routine, and mom would try to put him to bed drowsy but awake and after several nights, his bedtime routine had improved.   Finally, mom weaned down his nighttime feeds and Sean was finally sleeping through the night.

The Best Baby Sleep Book

2

Milk Allergy and Milk Intolerance

Milk protein intolerance and milk protein allergy are quite common in infancy. They are often overlooked and not diagnosed in a timely fashion. Lets look at a very common scenario:

Jonathan was never an "easy baby." From the day his parents took him home from the hospital, things were not easy for anyone. Jonathan cried incessantly and no matter what his parents did, he was extremely difficult to soothe. He was taken to the pediatrician several times, eventually to multiple pediatricians, and given a multitude of diagnoses and labels, none being correct or helpful. He spit up frequently, being dismissed by some as "normal" and being labeled by others as a reflux baby. He was started on an acid blocking medication with no significant improvement. Later, a label of colic had been used with a shoulder shrug and a half reassuring "he'll grow out if it."

His parents tried all possible treatments for colic including gripe water, a swing, driving around in a car for naps and to get him to sleep. Nothing helped. Mom and dad had tried the Cry It Out method and followed it to the letter without any success. They tried lactose free formulas without success. They even tried low iron formulas against the warning of their pediatrician[1]. Jonathan had other minor issues such as an occasional patch of eczema and cheeks that were always dry and red. The only thing that his parents had not tried was suppositories because Jonathan was the opposite of constipated, he frequently had loose stools, occasionally with mucus. When I saw Jonathan for the first time, he was 6 months old, about 2-3 months older than when most infants outgrow colic.

Not only was Jonathan a terrible napper and night sleeper, he was cranky all day from being tired, had a significant case of eczema, and a terrible diaper rash from his frequent stools. I checked a stool sample for microscopic blood with a bedside test called a 'Guiac'

---

[1] Low Iron Formulas are not to be used in infants as their use provides no benefit, and predisposes the infant to Iron Deficiency Anemia

which was immediately positive. We started Jonathan on a hypoallergenic formula specifically designed for milk protein sensitivity, and I instructed the parents that I would see them back in a week to reevaluate after a week on this formula. The next week, Jonathan was a new baby! His eczema was still there, but significantly better, his mood had improved, and there was no more blood in his stool. He still had some sleep issues due to the inconsistent routine, but with some structure, was able to sleep through the night in no time!

Jonathan's story is not uncommon. Milk protein intolerance and milk protein allergy are very real, common phenomena. They do not always show obvious signs and often present with just a cranky baby. It can occur in breastfed infants as well as formula fed ones. In breast-fed infants, it is actually the cows milk protein in moms diet that passes through the breast milk and effects the infants digestive tract. The sensitivity to this milk protein can cause the infants immune system to work overtime and may be associated with other phenomena such as asthma, eczema, or allergies.

It is not uncommon for milk protein intolerance to be confused for reflux, because the infants unfavorable reaction to the formula often causes frequent spitting. These infants can be labeled as colicky and are often misdiagnosed as reflux.

Milk protein intolerance can occur anytime from birth to 6 months of age. If this sounds like your baby, a trial of hypoallergenic formula may be what your baby needs. These hypoallergenic formulas are available in the supermarket and pharmacies without a prescription. I tell parents that they can expect to see one of two things when they start a hypoallergenic formula: a dramatic improvement, or no change at all. Commonly, parents call me after several days and tell me that they feel like they have a new baby!

SIGNS OF MILK INTOLERANCE

✓ Cranky and fussy
✓ Frequent liquid stools
✓ Blood or mucus in the stool
✓ Frequent spitting up
✓ Eczema
✓ Previous episodes of wheezing

You may ask your pediatrician to do a office test called a Guiac (Ga-Wa-Yak) on the stool to look for microscopic blood in the stool even if you do not see any blood in the diaper.

The good news for parents of infants with milk protein sensitivity is that most infants outgrow this sensitivity and can safely transition to whole milk on heir first birthday. Those that have difficulty doing this should be referred to an allergist.

What if I am breastfeeding and I think my baby has milk protein intolerance? How do I find out without stopping breastfeeding?

Remove the dairy and soy out of moms diet. The milk protein in the breast milk comes from the mom's diet. The milk protein being referred to is *cows milk protein*, not human breast milk protein. Infant milk formulas are made of cows milk with the fat removed (skim milk), essential fats added using more digestible oils, and adding vitamins and minerals such as Vitamin D and Iron. If a baby is intolerant of the formula, it is from the cows milk *protein* in the formula. If you want to continue breastfeeding, simply remove dairy and soy products from your diet.

What is hypoallergenic formula?

Hypoallergenic formula is regular formula with the cows milk protein broken down into such small pieces that the immune system has trouble recognizing it, and the digestive system cannot be irritated by it. It tastes quite different from regular formula, so don't be too surprised if your little one resists the change initially.

What about Soy?

25% of infants who have Milk Protein Intolerance also have a Soy Intolerance. Standard practice is to switch to a hypoallergenic formula and wait for a response. If there is improvement, Soy may be phased back in later with a watchful eye for recurring symptoms. Many years ago, it was standard practice to switch to a soy formula first. As increasing awareness of milk protein intolerance came about, the standard of care evolved to switching directly to a hypoallergenic formula, as opposed to soy.

Is it Lactose Intolerance?

Lactose intolerance in infants is rare. Lactose is a sugar present in milk. Lactose free formulas are available but may not improve any symptoms in your child except in special situations that are beyond the scope of this book. Milk intolerance in infants is due to milk *protein*, and not milk *sugar*.

What is the difference between Milk Protein *Allergy* and Milk Protein *Intolerance*?

Milk Protein **Allergy** is an immune response to the cows milk protein, which may be associated with rashes such as hives, eczema, fussiness and even wheezing when an infant or child is exposed to milk.

Milk Protein **Intolerance** is inflammation and irritation of the infant digestive tract due to exposure to cow's milk protein.

Both are treated the same way, with avoidance of cow's milk protein; either by limiting cow's milk from moms diet, use of a hypoallergenic formula, or both.

Severe Milk Protein *Allergy* may be associated with other food allergies, such as soy, wheat, and nuts. An evaluation for other allergies and a referral to a Pediatric Allergist should be considered.

3

Colic

Nothing is more frustrating for a parent than a fussy baby that won't stop crying. Colic is a word that is thrown around by doctors and parents, with few knowing exactly what it is. Colic is defined by a baby 2 weeks to 4 months old that cries excessively, often at the same time each day, with no specific reason. Frequently, a baby that cries excessively may be tired, overtired, and have a difficulty falling asleep. Fortunately, colic usually subsides by 3-4 months, around the time sleep training should start. A cranky baby past 4 months of age is *probably not colic*.

When Allison's parents brought her home from the hospital, she seemed to be a tranquil baby. She ate well, slept most of the time, and the first 2-3 weeks were uneventful. Toward the end of the first month, Allison became increasingly difficult. She would cry much more frequently and nothing that her parents could do would seem to soothe her. They would feed her, to no avail. They would change her diaper, but there was no effect. They would swaddle her, sing to her, but still no improvement. Allison had a decent amount of gas, and the crying actually got worse as the weeks rolled on. It became routine to hear Allison's shrill cry toward the evening, when she typically became out of sorts. When she was not having crying fits, she was a very cute baby, who was developing nicely, smiling, cooing, and gaining weight well. There was no spitting up, no bowel problems and no rash. Her pediatrician had tried changing the formula without any effect, and also had tried some acid blockers for possible "subtle reflux" with absolutely no effect. The only things that seemed to calm Amy down was to turn on the vacuum cleaner, and swinging in an infant swing. At around the 3rd month, the crankiness and crying began to subside and Allison became "easier." Her nighttime routine no longer consisted of constant crying, and she became a better napper. Once an appropriate routine was implemented she began to sleep through the night around 4 months of age.

What is a colicky baby?

A colicky baby is one that cries more than an average baby should. Your average 2 week old will cry about 2 hours per day total. Your average 6 week old cries about 3 hours a day, and your average 3 month old will cry about 1 hour a day. Most experts agree that a colicky infant cries more than 3 hours a day more than 3 days a week. This is known as the "rule of 3's." The quality of the crying is different. It's a harsher, different tone, not a hungry, wet, or tired cry. Many will describe colic as an "attack" and a baby will seem "tense" during the episodes.

Colic can only be diagnosed when other treatable possibilities, such as reflux or milk intolerance has been excluded.

COLIC
✓2 weeks to 4 months of age
✓Excessive crying, usually with no specific reason
✓More common in the evening
✓Different kind of cry
✓Difficult to soothe

"Is it gas? I think his tummy hurts!"

This is possibly the most common phrase I hear from new parents. While it is true that colicky infants have more gas, it is also true that if an infant cries for *any reason*, they will swallow more air, which will eventually go out the other end, causing more gas. We do not know exactly what causes colic. Some experts think it's an inability of an infant to cope with multiple stimuli, while other experts think colic is some form of abdominal pain.

Ok, I think my baby has colic. Now what?

If milk protein intolerance and reflux has reasonably excluded, and your baby has a diagnosis of colic, there are some measures you can take to lessen the burden of the excessive crying associated with colic.

Many different treatments for colic have been attempted, and unfortunately, there is no cure, or even an effective treatment for colic.

Probiotics (good bacteria) are currently being studied with some promise for colic relief. More studies need to be done to determine if there is a true benefit. Please keep in mind that the manufacturing of Lactobacillus (which can be obtained over the counter) is not regulated by the FDA.

What is "Gripe Water?"

Gripe water is a mix of water and herbs, mostly dill, that is touted as a cure for colic. Of all the remedies for colic, it is by far the best marketed, as you can find it for sale in popular baby stores and pharmacies. There is no "standard" or "original" gripe water, and there is no evidence that gripe water actually helps colic. In my experience, there is no benefit to use of gripe water. If you are going to try it, use a mass produced brand to increase the level of quality control.

Breastfeeding Techniques:

Letting your baby feed longer on one breast has been shown to decrease colic symptoms. It is thought to decrease the amount of swallowed air, thus decreasing gas pain.

Bottle-feeding Techniques:

Use of an upright curved bottle and bottles that use collapsible plastic bags has also been shown to decrease colic symptoms. There are commercially available bottles that allow for free flow of milk without a vacuum which can alleviate some symptoms.

Swaddling

Some infants are "swaddle friendly" and some are not. If you little one is colicky, swaddling is always worth a try. Being wrapped up tightly, is thought to replicate being in the womb, as the baby cannot move around just like in the last trimester. It makes them feel secure and can calm some fussy babies. While some babies respond quite well to swaddling, some simply will not tolerate. If your little one gets fussy and even more cranky after being swaddled, do not push the issue, and consider your baby not the swaddling type.

White Noise

Having grown up in the suburbs, I was used to living in a quiet house on a quiet street. My wife, a born and raised in New Yorker, had never known such quiet. When we went away for a weekend in the county, she could barely sleep because of the lack of background noise. Your baby experiences the same thing the first couple of weeks of life. Imagine for the last 9 months, you hear mom's heartbeat, all of mom's conversations, move around when mom moves around, and all in a very unpredictable manner. Now imagine you abruptly move to the much quieter county. You no longer hear moms heartbeat constantly when you fall asleep or when you wake up. White noise, or even heartbeat recordings may help your baby acclimate to the quieter, more predictable outside world. The noise of a vacuum cleaner, a radio set between two stations, and white noise CD's may be worth a try. White noise is a harmless thing to try. Your baby will not grow to depend on white noise, and may improve with it.

Infant swing

Some colicky babies respond very well to motion, especially infant swing motions. Often, parents of very colicky babies will tell me that the only thing that calmed their baby down was being in an infant swing. When my very colicky son was 2-3 months old, the swing was the only thing that would calm and soothe him. In fact, it worked so well, we purchased a swing to keep at each relative's house. Again, not all babies respond well to swinging motion, but of all the colic interventions I have seen (and tried), the infant swing by far has produced the most consistent results for me and my patients.

A vibrating bassinet can provide for sensory stimulation that can calm a colicky baby. In my experience, they are not as beneficial as the swing, but can provide significant relief for some babies.

> ## WHAT TO DO FOR COLIC
> ✓Swaddling
> ✓White noise (vacuum cleaner)
> ✓Infant Swing
> ✓Feeding techniques

4

Sleep Training and Illness

Colds, ear infections and other intermittent illnesses can be a challenge to even the best of sleepers, especially young infants. If your little one has a runny nose, a fever, cough, or congestion, she will be uncomfortable and may not be able to sleep very well. This is frequently where the routine falls apart. Parents often ask me how to handle a cold or ear infection before they begin sleep training, in the middle of sleep training, or after their baby is completely sleep trained.

Illness prior to Sleep Training

If you are about to start sleep training and your baby comes down with the sniffles, a cough or a fever, it is best to hold off and try to keep them as comfortable as possible without attempting to implement any changes. Frequently, the child will be rightfully cranky and their schedule may depend on how long the pain reliever/fever reducer lasts (usually 3-5 hours).

Illness in the middle of Sleep Training

If your child is in the middle of sleep training and gets a cold or ear infection, try not to abandon the routine that you have already established, but don't push too hard if your child is miserable. It's OK to allow for some breakdown in the routine. You may need to hold your baby and rock him to sleep if he is uncomfortable just so he can get some rest. Babies with colds and congestion have a much harder time falling asleep because they have to breathe through a stuffy nose. Infants under 4-6 months of age only breathe through the nose, so a stuffy nose can be particularly bothersome. Saline drops for the nose or a nasal aspirator may prove helpful in this age group.

Babies older than 6 months of age can breathe through the mouth, so a cold or a stuffy nose, although bothersome, may not affect sleep as significantly as it would in a younger baby.

Illness after Sleep Training

If you have worked hard and implemented sleep training with success and see its slipping away, do your best to maintain your routine, but don't be afraid to attend to your child's needs. If they are cranky in the middle of the night, especially with a fever, its ok to pick them up to console them. A little extra TLC will not negatively affect the sleep training, and should not be withheld when your child is under the weather. Most importantly, make sure that you immediately begin to implement your routine once you see your child turns a corner and begins to improve.

What about Diphenhydramine[2] (Benadryl)?

Diphenhydramine, is a safe and mildly sedating antihistamine. Parents frequently ask me about using it for various things, such as:

-Sleeping in a plane, or on a long car ride
-Helping to "jump start" sleep training
-Helping their child sleep during a cold or illness

Diphenhydramine is an antihistamine that is useful for allergies. It's quite safe, and its main side effect is mild drowsiness, which makes it helpful when your little one has trouble sleeping due to a cold.

It is reasonable for Diphenhydramine to be used during a cold or illness to help your child sleep comfortably. The American Academy of Pediatrics (AAP) advises against the use of cold medicines with the

---

[2] This is a generic name for a common pediatric antihistamine (one brand name is Benadryl)

exception of Diphenhydramine to help a child sleep and get some much needed rest in the midst of a cold. Always check with your healthcare provider regarding dosage.

I do not recommend that Diphenhydramine, or any other medication be used during sleep training. Infants need to make natural associations in their minds and understand how, why, and where to fall asleep. Diphenhydramine, however, does have a place in helping a child sleep when a cold or cough is keeping them up at night and nothing else seems to work. Some pediatricians suggest (or at least condone) its use in car and plane trips if one wants to use medication.

Diphenhydramine can make your child hyperactive

Keep in mind that one in 20 kids that are given Diphenhydramine become overexcited and hyper. If you are going to use Diphenhydramine for a long ride[3], I typically recommend doing a dry run the day before to make sure your child is not in that 5%. In addition, be sure to use the dye free version, as Red Dye #40 in standard preparations is well known to cause hyperactivity in some children.

---

[3] Please check with your physician before giving any medication to your child, even over the counter medications

Ear infections

An ear infection often occurs on the tail end of a cold. A child typically has a cough, a runny nose and then suddenly gets cranky, and may get a fever. If your baby is in the middle of a cold and all of a sudden wakes up cranky and has a temperature, there is a good chance that there is an ear infection, which will require antibiotics.[4]

Most 7-9 month olds will discover their ears and start playing with them, making their parents think that they have an ear infection, which is usually not the case. It is unlikely that a baby without a current or recent cold, without a fever, and in otherwise good spirits that just started playing with their ears has an ear infection.

Serious illnesses

If your baby has a serious illness and requires a hospitalization, this can wreak havoc on your routine. Often there is nothing you can do during the hospitalization except to make your baby feel as comfortable as possible. Depending on the nature of the illness, different tests at different times, medications, vital signs, and exams by doctors and nurses will make for a very difficult sleeping environment. After a hospitalization, parents may be

---

[4] Ear infections may resolve without antibiotics, and this is a viable option for children older than two. Younger children require antibiotics for ear infections.

nervous taking home a child and may feel more comfortable being extra attentive to a baby after such a stressful experience. It is not unusual for there to be a complete collapse of a sleep routine after a hospitalization.

When your little one comes home from the hospital, it is normal to experience significant anxiety. Feel free to hold your baby as much as you want, and as much as your baby wants. Try to phase your nighttime routine back in as soon as possible. A white noise machine, radio, or television noise in the background will help your baby readjust to the relatively quiet environment of your home. Try not to change the previous sleeping arrangements and return to the previous routine as soon as possible. Be patient and consistent, and your routine will return.

Teething

Teething usually occurs anytime from 6 months to 1 year. Most babies will have some level of discomfort associated with teething. Signs of teething include:
-drooling
-constant gnawing on just about anything
-low grade fever
-mild irritability

Most infants at the age of 3 months will begin to produce more saliva, and stick their hands in their mouths. This does not mean that teething is beginning.

It is a well accepted fact that teething can cause a *low grade* fever. Any temperature over 101.0 F means that you are likely dealing with an infection and not just with teething. If your baby has a rectal temperature over 100.4, especially before the age of 6 months, it is best to contact your healthcare provider.

You can help your child through teething by massaging the gums, giving them cold (not frozen) teething rings to chew on, and even a dose of Acetaminophen if nothing else works.

Topical gels and teething tablets are not helpful for teething. I discourage their use as they are not effective. Studies have shown than topical numbing gels get washed away by saliva in a matter or seconds.

Part II:

Behavioral

Imagine if every lunch you have ever had was a peanut butter and jelly sandwich. Now imagine without any notice or warning, you are given a salad for lunch, and you are not able to voice any protest because you do not know how to speak, and do not have the motor skills to make yourself a PB & J. The only response that you have at your disposal, is to cry. How do you think you would react when your lunch was changed so drastically without warning? Personally, I would cry. This is how your baby may feel when you attempt any kind of behavior modification program, including sleep training.

The methods that follow in the second part of this book are proven to work, and are gentler than the well known "Cry-it-out" method, but they are all changes in the routine of an infant or child, and will naturally be met with some resistance. It should be expected that some crying, whining, and challenges will occur along the way. Perhaps the most important advice for any sleep training, or even parenting in general, is that *consistency is required for any kind of behavioral modification.* Both parents and caregivers need to be on the same page, and everyone need use the same techniques in the same way. When you are ready to embark on sleep training, always keep in mind that consistency is the cornerstone of any sleep training program. Infants and toddlers thrive on structure. They feel anxiety when their schedule is not predictable. When a change occurs in an infant's schedule, it will usually be met with some degree of resistance; this is normal. If you provide loving, and consistent guidance for your little one, you will achieve results.

5

How To Put Your Baby To Sleep

Tommy was a sweet, lovable, 8 month old baby, with two very exhausted parents. Tommy was up 3-4 times a night, every night, ever since he his parents had brought him home from the hospital. They had been told by relatives that it was normal at 1 month of age, and just to "tough it out" with the hopes that sleep would prevail when he turned 4-6 months. Unfortunately, no one had told them how to get Tommy to sleep through the night. Tommy was rocked to sleep in his parents arms every night. Often times he would fall asleep breastfeeding. Mom and dad would transfer their sleeping angel ever so gently into the crib, only to hear him 2-3 hours later. Tommy's parents would take turns attending to him in the middle of the night. They would pick him up, rock him, cuddle him, feed him and help him drift off to sleep. This would happen again, and again, with no end in sight. While Tommy was a happy, thriving, delightful baby, the size of his parents coffee cups were ever increasing, and something needed to change.

A predictable consistent routine is essential for sleep training. Infants and toddlers are creatures of habit, and a predictable routine will decrease anxiety, make the child feel safe and secure, and will set you up for success.

The wind-down

Its important to include a wind-down for your little one, to make the transition from fun wakefulness to calm sleepy-time. The routine should be predictable, sedate, and calm. Dim the lights, play nice lullabies, try to fit in a relaxing warm bath, and give a nice warm bottle to help your little one transition to sleepy-time. A baby massage may help as well, with or without baby lotion. Regardless of what you choose for your routine, keep it consistent. Make sure that if you are not the only caregiver, that other caregivers do things the same way.

No baby sleeps through the night

Of all the factors that influence your child's ability to sleep through the night, the most important one is the nighttime routine. Inappropriate routine is the source of most behavioral sleep issues.

No baby actually sleeps through the night. There are babies that will wake up and go back to sleep on their own, and there are babies that wake up and cry, prompting you to come get them, go back to sleep with help, and then wake up at the end of another 2-3 hour cycle. The difference between these babies is the ability to self soothe. Self soothers do not need any help falling back asleep when their sleep cycle resets. Much of this has to do with temperament, with some infants simply being "easier" than others. However, with the proper routine, most, if not all, infants will be able to sleep through the night if you set them up properly.

Put your baby down drowsy, but awake

Lets say you fall asleep on your couch, and wake up in your hallway, or even your front yard, it would freak you out, wouldn't it? This is no different from what happens with an infant. The most common mistake I see is that parents rock the child to sleep and when the child is fast asleep in moms arms, they are then placed ever so gently into their crib.

In order to get your little one to sleep through the night, you must put them in the crib drowsy, but awake.

Lets look at it from the babies perspective…

Nowhere in the mind of the infant does the thought "wow, mom really looks tired" ever come to mind.

This concept seems foreign to most people, but makes perfect sense if you look at the most common mistake with the routine through the eyes of an infant. Infants are not manipulative, they only do several things: eat, poop, sleep and interact with mom and dad. If something does not please them, they cry and get attention. As they cry in the middle of the night, and you rush to the rescue, an association develops between their crying and their comfort.

If you continue to reinforce this behavior, you will only strengthen the association and make the habit of requiring soothing more difficult to break.

The most important part of sleep training is to make sure that when you put your baby down to sleep, they must still be awake and they must be in the exact same environment in which they will awaken. If your baby falls asleep in their crib in a darkened room thinking: "aaahhh, this is nice and cozy," then when she wakes up in a darkened room several hours later, there will be no change in the environment, and no crying. She will go back to sleep without waking you up.

Does this mean I have to stop holding my baby as much?

No. Please keep in mind that you cannot hold your infant enough and you cannot give them too much love. I am NOT telling you to leave them in the crib and let them cry until they pass out! I am trying to allow you to understand how your baby thinks, and why they are crying and waking you up. With this greater and deeper understanding, you will be able to properly handle bedtime routines and middle of the night awakenings.

What if my baby refuses to fall asleep in the crib?

This is usually the biggest hurdle that parents have to clear prior to successful sleep training. Try to put your baby down right after feeding when they are starting to look drowsy. You can stay near and pat them, sing them a lullaby, make a quiet "shhhhh" sound, or do whatever you usually do to soothe your baby, but your little one needs to be lying in the crib *before* he or she falls asleep.

What if my baby won't go into the crib at bedtime? I try to put him down but he cries the minute I try to put him down!

If your baby refuses to be in the crib at bedtime and begins to cry the moment you put him down, a great trick is to feed him his last bottle in the crib. The last bottle/feed of the day is a soothing, comforting, and bonding experience for you and your baby. Initially, you can start the feed holding your baby, and then, in the middle of the feed, put them in the crib and finish the bottle. I do not recommend that the baby takes a bottle lying down, but you can prop the baby up with one hand and hold the bottle with the other hand. Burping can also be accomplished with the child sitting up. You can try to burp your baby if they usually burp, but don't worry about it if they are already in the crib and about to snooze.

Most babies will get tired and doze off toward the end of the feed. Feeding them in the crib will create a comfortable, pleasant association with being in the crib. One of my patients, a 17 month old girl, would scream bloody murder every time mom and dad even approached the crib while holding her. They tried feeding her in the crib in the middle of the feed, which confused her a little, but she went with it, and on day 2, they had the bottle waiting for her in the crib. She actually asked to go into the crib to drink because she was anticipating a pleasant experience. She drank her bottle, snuggled in, and then drifted off to sleep without any fuss. When she would wake up several hours later, it was not as much of a surprise to wake up in the crib, because it was the same place she fell asleep. The parents even made it fun by having her favorite toy, her stuffed monkey, holding the bottle in the crib[5].

What if I am breastfeeding? How can I feed my baby in the crib?
Breastfeed, and transfer to crib

For moms that are breastfeeding, this situation gets a little trickier since the last feed has to take place outside of the crib and in moms arms. This defeats the entire purpose of having the child fall asleep in the crib. Many moms have told me that they are not happy with giving up the last feed to a bottle because they work during the day, and this bonding experience is something they look forward to all day. My recommendation in this case is to breastfeed as usual, and just as your baby is getting tired and towards the end of the feed, place the baby in the crib prior to her falling asleep.

Breastfeed, transfer to crib, feed expressed breast milk

If your baby falls asleep at the breast and you have trouble transferring her into the crib awake before the end of the feed, try to have several ounces of breastmilk pumped and standing by so that halfway through the feed,

---

[5] Children under 12 months of age should not have toys or stuffed animals in their crib due to the risk of SIDS.

you can transfer the baby into the crib and finish the feed in the crib with expressed breastmilk.

Transition from breastfeeding to bottlefeeding expressed breastmilk

If your baby does not like taking expressed breastmilk from a bottle, you will need to get her used to it before you try to manipulate the routine. If you wait until your baby is very hungry (a good rule of thumb is 15-20 mins after her usual feed) and then offer the bottle with expressed breastmilk, most babies will not argue about where the milk is coming from.

Beware of switching rapidly from breastmilk to formula.

If you are breastfeeding and are planning to try this technique, you will meet significant resistance if you switch from breastfeeding to bottle-feeding with *formula*. I strongly recommend that you give expressed breast milk in the bottle in this case due to the fact that babies who are used to breast milk dislike formula. I will never forget how much my son vomited when I gave him his first bottle of formula at 2 months of age. If your milk supply is dwindling, you need to supplement with formula, or you are planning on stopping breastfeeding, you can transition to formula from breast milk. If your baby gets used to drinking from a bottle with expressed breastmilk, it will be that much easier to transition from breast milk to formula.

Tooth Care

If you are feeding you little one in the crib and they have teeth, there is concern about milk bottle cavities. One a baby gets teeth, they should be cleaned daily. Cavities are the most common disease of children, and teeth that are not properly cleaned after drinking milk can quickly develop milk bottle cavities. If you feeding the last feed of the day in the crib, it is wise to feed an ounce of water right after the milk or to gently wipe the teeth with a damp washcloth. Several days of bottle feeding will probably not produce any cavities, so if you are bottle feeding in the crib as a transitional technique to soothe your baby in the middle of the night, it's not a big deal to clean the teeth or to follow it with water if it's only going be several days. However, if you consistently feed your baby in the crib, make sure to clean the teeth so that milk bottle cavities do not develop. Toothpaste and vigorous brushing are not necessary. If your little one resists tooth cleaning, try to do it several times a day apart from bedtime to get him used to it. The last thing you want during sleep training is to do something to your baby right before they fall asleep that they will perceive as unpleasant.

Lets revisit Tommy from earlier. After their consultation, Tommy's parents had an good grasp of what was going on, and where they had gone wrong. They worked on their bedtime routine, and over the course of a week, Tommy was falling asleep on his own in the crib, and the awakenings were almost gone. When he did wake up in the middle of the night, his parents knew how to handle it, and would calm him, and pat him, and get him back to sleep without picking him up and taking him out of the crib. Tommy fussed in the beginning, but his parents had been warned that things may get worse before they get better, so they were prepared for increased fussing and whining in their quest to keep their son in the crib. Soon Tommy began sleeping completely through the night for 12 hour stretches.

Key Points

✓It's important to wind-down your baby with a predictable routine.

✓No baby actually sleeps through the night, there are self soothers and those that require soothing.

✓Put your baby down drowsy but awake.

✓If your baby does not want to go into the crib, create a pleasant association by giving the last bottle in the crib.

6

How To Ditch The 3 AM Feed

Bradley was a healthy, happy, 8 month old boy, with a very exhausted mother. Bradley's mom could not understand why he was so hungry and could not sleep through the night. Bradley was not a particularly difficult baby, he did not spit up, was always in good spirits, did not have a trace a colic, and he loved to eat. This being her second baby, Bradley's mom was familiar with appropriate nighttime routine, and the concept of having a baby fall asleep in the crib. Since he was 3 months old, Bradley would fall asleep in the crib by himself after breastfed. When he was almost done with the feed, she would, making sure that he was still awake, place him gently in the crib and he would soothe himself to sleep without incident. The problem would always occur three hours later, when Bradley would "wake up and cry for food." Mom would pick him up and breastfeed him. This would repeat two to three times a night.

If you are like Bradley's mom, and use the phrases "he needs to eat" and "he wakes up hungry" as you sleepwalk toward the crib with a bottle in hand, then you are most likely dealing with trained night feeding, otherwise known as learned hunger. After the age of four months, no healthy baby requires a middle of the night feed.

When I am watching my favorite TV show, I like to have a bag of chips. My wife tells me that I don't need them, I know I don't need them, but it's such a habit that the experience of watching my show feels incomplete without my snack. Popcorn at the movies, hot dogs at a baseball game, and your morning cup of coffee all have something in common with your baby's middle of the night feeds, they are all habits. They are all learned behaviors that are part of our routines.

In the womb, babies get their nutrition continuously. After birth, feeds are quite frequent (every 1-3 hours) because their stomach is small and cannot hold enough calories to sustain them for more than several hours. As they grow, so does the stomach, and after about 4-6 months, the growth rate slows (in comparison to the first 4-6 months). At 4 months, a healthy infant no longer requires a feed in the middle of the night. If your baby is older than 4 months and wakes up to eat, it is out of habit and not out of necessity. This phenomenon is called "trained night feeding."

There are two types of trained night feeding, *breast feeding*, and *bottle feeding*.

Overcoming Trained Night Feeding with bottle feeding

If you have already mastered the nighttime routine and your baby is still waking up several times a night expecting a bottle, your next step will be to slowly decrease the volume of formula of each feed. Some infants respond quite well to this, and some are more stubborn than others. I typically recommend bringing the volume of the feed down 1 ounce per feed. For example, if your baby usually takes a 6 ounce bottle at 3 am, the next time he wakes up, give him 5 ounces. The next time he wakes up, try 4 ounces. Some babies will respond very well to this and can go faster than an ounce a feed, and some are more resistant and you may have to go down by half an ounce for a couple of days. Eventually, you will be able to simply give up the nighttime feed and your baby will begin to sleep through the night. If you decrease the volume and your baby resists, back up and a little bit and try again slower.

I am down to one ounce of milk but my baby just does not want to give it up!

If your little one refuses to let go of this last ounce of milk, take a half an ounce of milk and mix it with half an ounce of water. Do this for several days, and then transition to pure water. At this point, you can leave a sippy cup of water in the crib. It wont spill because of the buffer. If your little one wakes up expecting a short swig of water, they will not bother you if its readily available.

Overcoming Trained Night Feeding while breast-feeding.

Overcoming trained night feeding while breast-feeding is a little more complicated. Not only are you dealing with learned hunger, but you are also dealing with your baby's dependance on the entire breastfeeding experience, which also includes skin to skin contact and bonding with mom. For moms that have trained night feeding associated with breastfeeding, there is an extra step that needs to be taken to resolve this issue.

Initially, breast feeding trained night feeding needs to be transitioned to trained bottle feeding night feeding. You can still breastfeed but you will need to feed expressed breast milk from a bottle during the nighttime awakenings. This transition is often difficult but stick with it, if your baby truly thinks she is hungry, she will take the bottle. It may take several tries and several nights, but she will eventually take the bottle.

If you are weaning your baby's night feeding, and you meet resistance, slow down. If your baby is ok with going from 6 ounces to 4 then to 2 and then none, great! If you decrease the volume and your baby resists, back up and a little bit and try again slower.

What if I don't want to give up breastfeeding?

You do not need to give up breastfeeding. I am guessing that since you are reading this book, you are not too fond of the middle of the night feed, which is all we are trying to get rid of. You can breastfeed during any other feed. Since the goal here is to sleep through the night, we want to make the middle of the night feeds to be less of a fun experience.

What about putting rice cereal in the bottle?

Everyone has tried to put rice cereal in the bottle of the last feeding to help a baby stay full longer in an attempt to have them sleep through the night, but this does not work. Infants that wake up to feed do not wake out of hunger, they wake up out of habit. To stop this awakening, you need to break the habit, not increase the calories of the last bottle.

The Best Baby Sleep Book

7

How To Handle Middle Of the Night Awakenings

So you've mastered the nighttime routine, and your baby falls asleep by himself. You think you are getting somewhere, and you hear crying at 3 am. You walk into your baby's room, and your baby is holding out his arms, asking to be picked up. You approach the crib, and lay him down gently, patting him, soothing him, speaking in a hushed, comforting voice, but he won't budge. He keeps crying and crying. You don't want to pick him up as he will expect it the next time. What do you do?

Behavioral sleep training has two basic parts. Putting your baby to sleep the right way, and responding correctly when they wake up in the middle of the night. If you pick your baby up in the middle of the night, game over. He will expect you to pick him up the next time and the next. So what do you do when your crying baby expects you to pick him up at 3 in the morning, and won't t take no for an answer? The solution is to trade this big problem for a smaller one. A smaller problem that is much easier to solve.

If all else fails and your baby simply will not calm down, instead of picking him up, feed him a bottle in the crib. I known this goes against the trained night feeding, and that nutritionally, he does not need a bottle to sustain him. You are, in fact, creating another problem by doing this, and setting yourself for awakenings due to trained night feeding. However, you have to look at the priorities of sleep training. If you cannot get your infant to calm down and end up picking them up, not having to feed him in the middle of the night will not matter because he will wake up to be held. It is much easier to correct trained night feeding than it is to listen to your baby scream because they want to be picked up.

In addition, feeding your baby in the crib provides pleasant associations with being in the crib, which will facilitate less resistance at nap-time. The last thing you want at bedtime is an infant that dreads being in the crib. A baby that screams the second you put him into the crib, provides a stressful experience all around. The more pleasant the experience is, the easier all the transitions will become. When you get to the point where your baby is at ease in the crib, and only wakes up to feed out of habit, you can then slowly wean down the bottle as instructed in the trained night feeding section.

8

"Mommy, Will You Stay With Me?"

Nicholas was always a clingy baby. He loved to be held, and when his parents finally began to implement sleep training at 9 months of age, they did everything right. They mastered his nighttime routine and stopped rocking him to sleep. They weaned down his feeding and transitioned it to water. They then got him to drink from a sippy cup of water in the crib. Everything was textbook and should have worked for a baby 4-9 months of age, except for the fact that Nicholas, despite all of these advances, refused to allow mom or dad to leave the room. As soon as mom or dad came out of sight, he would start to whine and would not let them leave the room. Mom and dad were reduced to waiting for him to fall alseep and sneaking out quietly. Nicholas would wake up in the middle of the night and would not need a bottle or to be picked up, he just wanted mom or dad in the room. As long as they were in the room, he would be fine and drift off, but as soon as they would try to leave, he would cry and fuss, bringing them right back.

Now you see me, now you don't

Prior to 6-9 months, when something is out of sight of your infant, it is truly out of mind. This is because infants don't realize that when something is not in front of them, that something is missing. This is why playing peek-a-boo with your 3-4 month old is so fun, your baby simply cannot believe that you just reappeared out of nowhere. Around 6-9 months, your baby will begin to realize that things exist even if they are out of sight, and will get quite upset when mom or dad leave the room.

How do we fix it?

If your baby simply wants you in the room, you will have wean him off your presence, just like you weaned him off the bottle in the middle of the night. Instead of walking out and letting him cry, you will have to do it in small increments so he gradually gets used to an increasing distance between you and him.

This technique works well for older infants and toddlers who throw a temper tantrum when they want you in the room. Quick and drastic changes will not get you very far, as your baby will likely resist the changes and place you right back at square one.

As long as you make slow and gradual changes, your baby will not protest, just like when you wean down a bottle slowly.

Step 1: Make sure you have a smaller lighter chair where you can sit next to the crib.

Step 2: Move the chair a foot farther than the crib- change nothing else. Sit in the chair until your baby falls asleep.

Step 3: Continue to move your chair away from the crib by a foot each night. You will eventually reach the doorway. Keep the chair in the doorway for one night.

Step 4. Move the chair out of the doorway into the hallway. Keep the door open. Keep the lights in the hallway dim.

Step 5: Move out of sight and comfort with your voice gently if your baby starts to whine.

The Best Baby Sleep Book

9

The Last Straw Method For Resistant Toddlers

Joseph had just turned 18 months, and had never been a good sleeper. He was a healthy boy who had been rocked to sleep for almost his entire life. He woke up constantly and required a drink of milk two to three times a night. Joseph's family came to me exhausted and concerned for their family's sanity, as they were expecting another child in a month. The prospect of more than one sleepless child terrified them.

We went to work on the routine, and in several days, Joseph was falling asleep in the crib by himself. We worked on the trained night feeding, and in a week, Joseph had switched from milk in the middle of the night, to a sippy-cup of water left in the crib, which he could reach for and manipulate himself. He even told mom exactly where to leave the cup in the crib. He still needed mom to help him go back to sleep in the middle of the night, and she had slowly moved the chair from next to the crib to the open doorway. At this point, she could make no more progress. She could not move the chair further out of the room into the hallway. In addition, Joseph would cry in the middle of the night, and despite knowing exactly where the sippy cup of water was, he would cry until mom came in and physically placed the cup in his hands.

What happened here? Read the following example and you will see...

Paul was 18 months old. Twice a week, he would go to the grocery store with Dad as part of their usual routine. Every time they were at the store, Paul's dad would get him a cookie from the bakery and Paul would enjoy munching on it. One day, Paul's mom took him to the store, and as soon as they got in the store, Paul made a B-line for the bakery and pleaded (as eloquently an 18 month old can plead) for a cookie. Mom was not as permissive of sweets and said no. Can you guess what happened next?

At first glance, the two examples above could not look more unrelated, but they are both the exact same behavior, temper tantrums. Joseph is used to having attention from his parents in the middle of the night, and Paul is used to having cookies at the store. When there is a change, they react like any normal toddler, they throw a fit!

What do we do about temper tantrums?
Rules of dealing with temper tantrums:
1. Ignore them; *do not react*
2. Expect that it will get worse before it gets better

At this point, Joseph's crying in the middle of the night is nothing but a temper tantrum. This occurs as a result of the developmental stage of the child. Temper tantrums usually peak at around 15-21 months, but can be seen in 2,3 and 4 year olds. When you implement sleep training past 15 months, you may run into this issue. Tantrums interfering with sleeping through the night are dealt with like any other temper tantrums, by withholding attention and not letting your child win.

How do we handle sleep training in the temper tantrum prone group?
First you will need to implement the behavioral techniques presented earlier, in the order they are presented. The routine has to be appropriate, and there can be no more trained night feedings. If you have accomplished all of this, and are in the same situation as Joseph's parents, with a toddler who depends on your

attention, you will need to treat this issue just like a temper tantrum, and accept that at this point of sleep training, the developmental stage will not allow for a quiet exit

This sounds like the Cry-it-out method. Does every toddler need to cry it out for results?

Absolutely not. This is what I call the "last straw" method. Once every behavioral issue has been addressed, and we are left with a middle of the night temper tantrum, you will have to allow the temper tantrum to run it's course without appeasing it.

If Paul's mom gave in to the tantrum and gave him the cookie, how much success do you think she would have keeping the cookie out of Paul's mouth during the next trip to the grocery store? Not too much. However, if Paul's mom chose to stand her ground and not allow the tantrum to control her, then the next visit to the store may not be so bad.

Once we understood that the last issue we had to deal with was Joseph's middle of the night tantrums, his parents, were much better equipped to deal with them. In the middle of the night, his parents would allow him to fuss for 5 minutes before firmly telling him that it was bedtime. They were given strict instructions not to cave in to his demands.

Trying to negotiate with a tired toddler in the middle of a temper tantrum is the equivalent of negotiating with a terrorist. Do your best to ignore the behavior and not to react. If one parent usually caves in, try to have the non-caving parent be the one to deal with the middle of the night tantrums.

The best way to understand how to deal with middle of the night attention seeking temper tantrums is to realize that your child is not hungry, not thirsty, and only wants one thing: for things to stay the same. They want you in the room at 3 in the morning because it's is what they are used to, it's what they expect, and a change is not welcome. You are reading this book because you want a change.

This is a game of chicken. You toddler will cry and fuss because they prefer the status quo, and you will need to do is to show them that crying and fussing are not appropriate ways of getting what they want. This is different from crying it out, because the CIO method aims to teach an infant how to self soothe by placing them in a situation in which they have no choice but to learn. A toddler that requires the "last straw" technique already knows how to self soothe, and does not eat out of habit. YOU are their habit. Be firm, and do not let them dictate the terms of the middle of the night awakenings.

.

10

To Cry Or Not To Cry (It Out)?

While certainly not for everyone, the Cry It Out (CIO) method is a widely used, albeit controversial, sleep training technique. This method has come under fire for being too harsh on the infant and mother. As a Pediatrician and an Infant Sleep Consultant, I often receive requests to provide an alternative to the CIO, and many inquiries my practice receives begin with "we tried the Cry-it-out but...."

For those parents who have the stomach to implement this method, it is quite effective in a fairly short period of time (usually within several days).

Those who should NOT use the CIO method:

-Parents that are unable to stick to it (an inconsistent CIO method will create more problems than it will solve)
-Children that make themselves vomit when they cry excessively
-Children that are ill (colds, ear infections, etc.) Sleep training should take place only with a child in good health. If you are unsure about your child's health status, please contact your pediatrician)
-Children under 4 months of age.

To implement the CIO method, you will want to have a quiet, comforting bedtime routine that helps wind down your infant. You will need to put your baby, drowsy but awake into the crib. There should be no rocking to sleep, and the baby should be awake when he is placed in the crib. Once you put the baby down, the next step is to leave the room, after which the baby will probably cry. According to the CIO method, you should hold off on going back into the room for approximately 3-5 minutes, afterwards, you can go back and soothe the baby *without picking him up*. If you pick him up, all your progress, and the crying you endured will have been for nothing. Soothe and pat your baby and then leave the room again, this time for a longer stretch (5-7 minutes). Repeat this again with increasing intervals until you hit 15-20 minutes. At some point, your baby should fall asleep. This may need to be done for several days, and rarely, weeks in a row.

This method is not for everyone, and if you cannot go through with the method to completion, then it's best to use an alternative method. Half hearted attempts at the Cry It Out method only cause stress with no benefits. If you feel uncomfortable with this method from the beginning, it is not for you.

There are some experts that now claim this method causes emotional problems and sets up the baby for emotional damage and problems such as ADHD and anxiety/depression. To date, there have been no studies and no scientific evidence that has validated such concerns.

The Best Baby Sleep Book

11

Naps

Nap training is the finer point of sleep training. If you are attempting to manipulate your infants nap schedule, then you should have already accomplished a nighttime routine, have your baby sleeping through the night and not have any awakenings. Nap training is not difficult and can be accomplished by gently and gradually manipulating your infants schedule.

Don't start Nap training until your baby sleeps through the night

One of the key differences between nap training and nighttime sleep training is that at night, no matter how poor the sleep routine and how fragmented the nighttime sleep is, a baby will not go all night without sleeping. Eventually, sleep *will* prevail wether in the crib, the car-seat, or in mothers arms. This is not the case with naps. A baby can miss a nap and move on (albeit,   not in the best mood). Napping has much more variability than nighttime sleep, and also is much more dependent on the baby, compared to nighttime sleep, where practically any baby can be trained to sleep like an angel.

Don't miss the window!
The first nap is the most important one of the day, as a tired cranky baby early in the day will set the tone for the rest of the day. Many parents describe this elusive "nap window" which is a time when your little one is able to quietly and calmly fall asleep, but is not cranky (yet). Pay careful attention to your babies "tired clues." Your baby will show you signs of wanting to sleep, from yawning, to stretching to making a characteristic noise. As soon as you see these signs, act immediately and get your baby ready for a nap. If you miss this window, your baby will get overtired, lose the ability to nap, and you will have a

overtired, hyper crankster that is hours away from the next nap.

Rooster Baby

Lets separate your infant into one of two types of sleepers. Is she a rooster baby or not?

A rooster baby will wake up at the same time every morning no matter what time they go to sleep. You put them to bed at 9 pm, up at 7am. Bed at 7pm, up at 7am... bed at midnight, up at 7am. These infants are a lot less flexible about when they nap. Since your baby finds it necessary to wake up at the same time every morning, that first nap will be rather inflexible, at least the start of the nap will be. You can, however, control the duration of the nap to help manipulate naps "downstream"

Lets look at how many naps your baby will take during the day. Most infants over 4 months take 2-3 naps a day. One early morning (usually the most important, and sets the tone for the day), midmorning, and late afternoon. Depending on the child, sometime later in the first year (usually around 9 months or so), the 3rd nap begins to get phased out and your baby will only be taking 2 naps.

The Cat-Napper.

Some infants are cat-nappers, babies who only grab about 30-45 minutes of sleep at a time when they nap. *Unless there is a specific medical problem that causes your child to wake from their nap after a short time, you cannot make a cat-napper sleep longer. You can shorten a child's nap, but you cannot prolong it.*

Change of Venue

Some babies prefer to nap in a different place, while some don't seem to care either way. If you have a baby that is resistant to napping in their crib, a change in scenery may be the key. Try using a pack and play in the living room or guestroom, or try taking a stroll. Some infants prefer motion sleep for their naps in contrast to sleeping in a crib. Rocking motions help soothe infants, especially fussy newborns, as it replicates the environment in the womb. Keep in mind, your baby slept while you were moving around during your pregnancy, and sleeping in a completely still environment is in itself a transition.

Too much light?

Napping during the day may be difficult if there is too much light in the room, as light provide clues to your baby that it is not sleepy time. This is not usually the case at night with the sun down, although street lights in a city may interfere with restful sleep as well. I took case of one family who lived in Times Square in Manhattan, and from the baby's window, you could actually see a gigantic lit up M&M (they lived on top of the M&M store). Needless to say, prior to any sleep training, the parents had to get black out curtains to block out the street light. Sometimes it may be necessary to use duct tape to seal the sides of the black out curtain to prevent light from creeping around the edges.

Temperament

You should always take your babies progress with a grain of salt and try not to force anything because your older child slept better or because your relatives tell you they should be sleeping a certain amount. People often forget to account for temperament, which is best described as an innate set of characteristics that contribute to your baby's overall persona. You may have a sensitive baby that needs a little more time to fall asleep and a little more cajoling, or you may have just as-stubborn-as-can-be baby that resists any noticeable change in routine, making transitions and shifts in the routine more difficult. Temperament is what people refer to when they say people have an easy baby or a difficult baby.

Not a great napper?

Is it a problem if your baby sleeps great at night but does not nap very well? No. Your child needs a certain amount of sleep, if they are happy and seem well rested, and grab most of their sleep during the overnight and just need a little during the day, this is not an issue to worry about. Certainly, if your baby is constantly tired and cranky, there may be more to it, and you should discuss it with your pediatrician.

Nap Training:

First nap

First, work on the first nap, this one is crucial to be successful. The last thing you want is to have an overtired baby by 10am, which will make for a loooong day. After the first nap is established, you can play around with second and third nap, depending on your child's abilities to nap and your schedule. Be in tune to your baby's tired clues and get her down for her first nap like clockwork. If you have a rooster baby, the timing of this first nap is usually inflexible.

Catnapper training

If you have a catnapper, then your nap schedule will likely be more rigid because you will not be able to manipulate the timing, and may have to build your schedule around the naps, have someone help you, or take the child with you and time the walk in the stroller or the ride in the car (that is, of course, if your little one responds to motion sleep).

Non-catnapper training

If you baby can take long naps, you may feel free to play around with the time to suit your schedule but cutting a nap short to provide for an earlier start for the next nap, or to move a nighttime bedtime either earlier or later.

- *Rooster babies need their first nap perfectly timed*
- *Catnappers are rather inflexible with moving around nap schedules and it's best to conform to their needs.*
- *Motion sleep can help you stay sane and provide for napping "on-the-go."*
- *Change of venue may help for nap resistant babies.*

Tired Cues

- Yawning
- Eye rubbing
- Fussiness not responding to eating
- Grunting
- Mouthing objects but not wanting to eat
- Jerking and flailing arm and leg movements
- Decreased eye contact
- Increased clenching of the fists

Trial and Error

Lastly, nap training and manipulation comes down to trial and error. If you try to keep your child up for an extra hour to phase their bedtime to a convenient hour later, and you get an incredibly cranky baby that you want to avoid at all costs, then don't do it again!

12

Prevention

The first two sections of this book are devoted to problem solving. The medical section addresses common medical issues that cause disrupted sleep, and can interfere with sleep training for your baby.

The behavioral section provides you with the tools to correct behavioral sleep problems such as a inappropriate routine, and trained night feeding.

This chapter is devoted to those parents with infants younger than 4 months. You cannot sleep train an infant younger than 4 months, but you can *set yourself up for success*.

As a pediatrician, my roots are in prevention, and I firmly believe that an ounce of prevention is worth a pound of cure. If you have a young infant and need help on preventing poor sleep habits from developing, if you are not sure how to set yourself up for success, or if you already see some of the problems developing and want to head them off at the pass, then this section is for you.

When parents use me as their pediatrician, they almost never have to utilize my sleep training services. They don't have to break the habit of a faulty routine, and they rarely have to implement a cry-it-out method. Sleep problems are not inevitable, and can be prevented prior to becoming problems. Behavioral sleep problems occur because small problems are not addressed when they begin, and eventually become big problems. The longer you let an unwanted behavior persist, the longer it will persist, and the stronger and more deep-rooted the behavior becomes. When you finally decide to do something about it, it inevitably becomes more of a battle.

Before I go any further, I want to point out that you cannot hold a baby enough, kiss him enough, hug him enough, or love him enough. The methods presented do not endorse any particular style of parenting. The information presented offers gives you guidelines to help facilitate your baby's learning how to self soothe, and how to avoid patterns that will inevitably lead to problems with sleep.

First 6 weeks

For the first 6 weeks, your baby's sleeping habits may be quite erratic, and are due to brain immaturity, the shock and adjustment of a new environment, and the need to eat frequently. There is no controlling or manipulating a newborns sleep habits, and you will have to attend to your baby around the clock to make sure that he is fed, changed, and comfortable. He will frequently fall asleep on you when you are feeding him, which is ok. Do not expect to teach your baby to self soothe during this period. Your baby is very immature and fragile at this age.

6 weeks to 3 and a half months.

At this point, you can begin to facilitate good sleeping habits. While you will probably not get results at this stage, you can lay the foundation for good sleeping habits.

Babies at this age are not always wet or hungry when they cry. They may be bored, tired, lonely, frustrated, or colicky. Often the cries are different, and caregivers at this stage can usually tell a bored cry from a hungry or wet cry. Try to differentiate the reason your baby is crying, and respond accordingly. Sometimes all that you will need to calm your baby is to put in a pacifier or to turn on a mobile. If you pick up your baby within seconds of every whimper, then an association will develop and it will be difficult for your baby to learn to self soothe.

Toward the end of a feed, if you see your baby getting sleepy, try to put him down before he falls asleep. It's not imperative that your baby goes down awake in this age group, but you should be aware of the importance of putting your baby down *drowsy but awake* as you approach the 4 month mark

3 and a half to 4 months:

In this small and critical period, while you may not achieve results of having your baby sleep through the night, it is the absolute best time to perfect your nighttime routine. Your baby may still need to wake up for a feed, but as you phase in your routine, and teach your baby how to fall asleep in the crib and not on you, you will set yourself up for success.

4 months:

At this point, you should have a nighttime routine, and your baby falls asleep on his own in the crib. He may still wake up for feeds. This is when you want to start sleep training and wean down night feeds as outlined in the trained night feeding chapter.

Set Yourself up for success

✓Put your baby down right before they doze off, or as they are falling asleep

✓If your baby begins to cry, listen to the type of cry (wet, hungry, soiled, bored) before immediately rushing to soothe him

✓Expect setbacks, do not get discouraged

✓Seek evaluation from your pediatrician if your baby fits the description of the common medical issues presented in this book

✓Seek help when you are too tired to follow through

✓Be consistent with your baby, (this means all caregivers do the same thing)

What You Must Avoid

✓Rock your baby to sleep in your arms day 1 through the end of the 3rd month, and then expect to start sleep training from scratch

✓Put off sleep training and say "I'll do it when he's older, so he will understand more." The longer you wait to sleep train, the more engrained the behaviors, and the stronger the associations become. The longer you wait, the more difficult it will become.

✓Picking your baby up at the first sign of the faintest whimper.

✓Assuming every time your baby cries, that he is hungry, and then feeding him

✓Get frustrated and take the easy way out when you hit a setback

✓Implement the techniques in this book out of order

✓Allow other caregivers to do things differently because "this is what worked for their baby."

✓Assume what worked for your previous child will work for this one

You can never hug, kiss, hold, or love your baby too much! The suggestions in this book only serve as guidelines to help your baby learn how to soothe themselves to sleep. These are simply guidelines drawn on techniques I have used over the years to achieve great success in getting thousands of children to sleep through the night. Every child is an individual, and if the guidelines are not working for your child, please bring your child to your pediatrician for further evaluation.

Infants and children are amazing. Having spent my career studying and working with them, not a day goes by that I am not left in awe at the amazing ability of young children to learn and adapt. Have faith in yourself, your parenting abilities, and your baby, and you will have a baby that truly sleeps like a baby!

13

Double Trouble: Sleep Training Multiples

Sleep training for twins and multiples may appear more challenging, but it does not have to be. Most sleep issues in twins can, and should be approached in the same way as an individual baby. There are, however, some special issues to take into account.

Special Considerations for Multiples

•CoSleeping

•Coordinated Sleep Schedules

•Identical vs Fraternal (non-identical) Twins

•When one wakes the other one up

CoSleeping:

Many parents place multiples (pictures of them head to head in a crib) in the same crib for the first several months. While co-sleeping was addressed earlier, and my stance (as well as the AAP's) stance is against co-sleeping, it is entirely reasonable, and common, for twins to be in the same crib for the first several months, provided some precautions are taken. The American Academy of Pediatrics (AAP) does not address co-sleeping multiples in the same crib.

Precautions:

Head to Head

Each twin should be placed "head to head" in the crib. Do not place them head to foot. Between 0-4 months, you may have them with or without a barrier. If you use a barrier, make sure it is a specific crib divider and not a makeshift one (especially not a pillow). Most infants begin to roll at 4 months of age, making it a hazard to have 2 infants in a crib capable on rolling into each other.

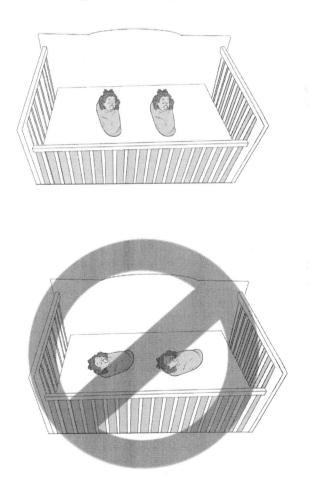

1-2 feet apart

Twins should not be touching and should be separated by at least 1-2 feet. Each should have his or her own space. You should have designated sides for each twin, and be consistent, so they get used to their own special place.

Routine SIDS precautions

All the routine SIDS precautions discussed earlier should be followed. Babies should sleep on their back, the room should be a comfortable temperature (68-74 degrees), and there should be no cigarette smoke. Since many multiples are born smaller and premature, there is an increased risk of SIDS due to these risk factors, which are beyond your control. Accounting for the SIDS risk factors that are within your control is even more important when dealing multiples.

Move them when they are ready

Each twin will need their own crib when they begin to move around and roll starting around 4-6 months. It is unsafe to have two babies rolling into each other in the same crib.

Coordinated Sleep Schedules

The key to sleep training twins and multiples is to coordinate their sleep and feeding schedule so that they are in sync from day one. This means putting them to sleep at the same time, feeding them at the same time, and if one wakes up a little earlier than the other, waking them at the same time. This often comes as second nature for identical twins, but fraternal (non identical) twins may take more work. If you are consistent from the beginning (not just the 4 month mark), having a common feeding, playing, and sleeping schedule will allow for easier sleep training.

Prior to 4 months of age, your goal with sleeping twins will only be to get them on a similar schedule. This should start as soon as possible to ensure success (and your sanity). It's hard enough to take care of 2 babies as once, let alone 2 babies with opposite schedules.

Identical vs Fraternal (non-identical)

Generally speaking, identical twins are easier to sleep train than fraternal. They tend to synchronize their schedule naturally and with greater ease. Fraternal (not identical) twins may or may not co-sleep well together, it depends on their personality. Identical twins tend to co-sleep very well together. Twins and multiples have higher rates of prematurity and associated complications such as reflux. If one twin has medical needs that may cause more frequent awakenings, this may hamper your sleep training.

When one wakes up the other - believe it or not, this is not a common problem, especially if bedtime routines are strictly followed. Twins typically respond well to a structured schedule and go into sync fairly quickly. In addition, infants do not usually get woken up by a siblings cry. Occasionally, a baby will be sensitive and frequently woken up by a sibling who has a different routine, in which case they will need to be in separate sleeping quarters. This is not a common scenario.

Twins and multiples have a higher rate of prematurity, which will effect the age that you can safely begin to sleep train. In my practice, I wait until the child is 4 months older than the due date, and has no significant medical or developmental issues.

Example: a set of twins that were born 2 months early should wait until they are 6 months old before sleep training.

14

Safe Sleep

Safe Sleep

Safe sleeping is vital to the health of your baby and your peace of mind. Since your baby spends 60-75% of their first year sleeping, it is paramount that safety become a priority during this time. Undeveloped muscle tone, an immature brain, and poor head control demand several basic safety precautions be taken.

Safe sleeping can be broken down into position, immediate environment, and general environment.

Position:

SIDS (Sudden Infant Death Syndrome) is a very real and important cause of infant death in the first year of life. SIDS may be a blanket term for several different illnesses yet to be identified that lead to the same outcome. While we do not know everything about SIDS, we do know that a significant percentage of cases can be avoided by putting your baby to sleep on their back. Ever since the American Academy of Pediatrics (AAP) began recommending this practice of back to sleep in 1994, the SIDS rate decreased dramatically. Sleeping on the side poses a risk of flipping onto the stomach if the baby moves a certain way.

Immediate environment

Other factors for a safe sleep environment include the environment where your baby sleeps. Environment can be divided into the immediate sleeping environment and then to the more general environment.

The Immediate environment where your baby sleeps is critical to safe sleeping practices. There should be no objects in the crib except your baby. No pillows, no blankets, no stuffed animals, no quilts, no crib bumpers.

The outfit:

I recommend either a sleepsack, nightgown, or footie pajamas. A good rule of thumb is that your baby should wear one extra layer than you are to feel comfortable. (If you feel comfortable in a T-shirt and pajama pants, you should put your baby in a onesie plusfootie pajamas. Some babies run a little hotter than others, so always reevaluate to make sure your baby is not too hot or too cold. If you baby sweats, odds are she's too hot. For very young babies (several days to weeks old), a hat may be used to help the baby maintain temperature. Bonnets and hats with strings should not be used.

The crib:

It is safest to use a solid, sturdy crib without a dropside. Dropside cribs have been associated with infants getting trapped between the crib and the mattress.

The Mattress:

Many crib mattresses are advertised as dual infant and toddler mattresses. One side is firmer for infants and the other is softer for after the first birthday. Make sure your mattress is turned to the correct side if you have one of these dual mattresses.

Crib Bumpers:

I have never liked crib bumpers, as they are unnecessary but seem to be a required accessory. It appears you can only buy a fitted sheet for a mattress accompanied by a comforter and a set of extra soft crib bumpers with a cute design on it. In theory, these crib bumpers are supposed to prevent your newborn from suddenly launching themselves into the hard bars of the crib and injuring themselves.

Fact: A newborn does not roll. Gross motor skills required for rolling are not present until 3 months at the earliest. It is highly unlikely that the cute bundle in your crib will suddenly roll so fast as to injure themselves on the bars.

Lets fast-forward to your 4-6 month old who has met the common developmental milestone of rolling. The very real risk of SIDS mandates that one not have any stuffed animals or pillows in the crib until the child is one year of age… does that not include a long thin pillow that surrounds the baby that now has the motor skills to actually roll face first into this pillow that surrounds them? As a new parent, I had crib bumpers in my sons crib until he was about 5 months old and I saw him roll face first into it and almost suffocate. The crib bumpers went in the garbage that night.

Older babies may actually use crib bumpers as a step after they learn to pull themselves up and fall out of the crib. At no point are crib bumpers a good idea.

EXTERNAL ENVIRONMENT

The external environment also plays a role in safe sleep.

Temperature

The temperature of the room where your baby sleeps in very important, as overheating has been implicated in SIDS. Set the temperature somwhere from 68-74 degrees, depending on how comfortable your baby feels, and how many layers he has on. If you cannot precisely control the temperature of the room, get a room thermometer and keep checking your baby to making sure she is not too hot or too cold. If your baby is sweating, odds are she is too hot. Make sure not to keep your baby in direct sunlight next to a window, unless you have been directed to do so by your doctor for jaundice reasons, as direct sunlight through a window can produce significant increases in temperature, and may predispose to overheating.

Humidity

Having adequate humidity in the baby's room is important, as too low humidity will dry out your baby's nose and make it uncomfortable to breathe. If you use a humidifier, make sure to change the filter frequently, as this is a favorite place for mold to set up shop. You should set your humidifier to 40-50% humidity.

Smoking

Cigarette and other tobacco smoke is not only detrimental to your health, but also to the health of your baby. Smoking has been linked to cases of SIDS, and places your baby at risk of asthma, and upper respiratory infections. I cannot tell you how many times parents tell me (in the office and in a house call setting) that they "never smoke around the baby" when I can smell the stale cigarette smoke the second I walk into the room. When you smoke, it permeates your hair, your clothes, and stays in your lungs for some time. Even if you go outside to smoke, not all the smoke particles stay outside. If a non-smoker can smell stale cigarette smoke on you, imagine what your baby can smell.

Pacifiers:

Use of a pacifier is recommended by the American Academy of Pediatrics as long as it does not interfere with breastfeeding. Infants are encouraged by the AAP to start using the pacifier at 1 month of age. It is thought that pacifier use increases the level of arousal, making SIDS less likely. Breastfeeding advocacy groups oppose use of pacifiers as they have the potential to interfere with breastfeeding by causing nipple confusion.

Home Monitors and Baby Alarms

Home video monitors that allow you to see your baby on a video screen when the baby is in a different room, are great and provide peace of mind. I used one for my son, and can attest to the secure feeling that one has when they glance onto the small monitor on their nightstand and see their baby sleeping peacefully.

Baby movement alarms are products that sense movement in your baby and alarm when movement is detected. These have not been proven to prevent SIDS, and in my experience, unnecessarily heighten anxiety by going off every time the baby moves.

Co-Sleeping

Whenever the topic of safe sleeping and sleep training is brought up, co-sleeping is often mentioned. Co-Sleeping is very controversial, as a consensus is has never been reached. Parts of Europe, Asia, Africa, South and Central America, just to name a few, not only condone, but encourage and endorse co-sleeping as the cultural norm. The American Academy of Pediatrics (AAP) discourages Co-Sleeping because it is a risk factor for SIDS. Studies have shown that co-sleeping has higher rate of SIDS than infants that do no share a bed. In addition, babies that sleep in the room with mom and dad in their own safe little area, such as a crib, basinet, or co-sleeper had the lowest risk of all. SIDS risk is highest when a parent falls asleep on a couch or chair holding the baby.

In my practice, I do *not* recommend that parents share a bed with their infants due to the increased risk of SIDS. My position is not only due to the studies, but from personal experience, as I was witness to a SIDS case that occurred in a 2 day old in a hospital nursery who was sharing a bed with a mother.

> ### Why not co-sleep?
> - Baby may get trapped between the mattress and the bedframe
> - An adult may roll onto the baby
> - Baby may get shifted on it's stomach
> - Suffocation hazard due to an inappropriately soft mattress, pillow or comforter.

Sharing a room

While co-sleeping is a risk factor for SIDS, sharing a room with your baby is preferred for the first 4-6 months, as it has been shown to decrease the risk of SIDS. At the 4-6 month mark, it may be difficult to keep your baby in the room and implement sleep training. Some infants are easier to sleep train than others, and may be more amendable to sleep through the night than others, in which case sharing a room may be continued past the 4-6 month mark. More difficult infants may need to sleep in their own room, or a part of the parents room where they cannot see mom and dad when they wake up. One family I took care of in Manhattan (where space is at a premium) used a chinese wall to partition a section of their bedroom.

SIDS Risk Factors Beyond Control
- Prematurity
- Low birth weight
- Young mom (under 20 years of age)
- Smoking during pregnancy
- Lack of prenatal care
- Brother or sister with SIDS

Controllable SIDS Risk Factors
- Sleeping on the belly (24 times higher risk than on back)[1]
- Sleeping on the side (15 times higher risk than on back)
- Overheating
- Sleeping on a soft surface
- Sleeping with soft items (pillows, stuffed animals)
- Use of "sleep positioner."

Co-Sleeping Safely

The following is not an endorsement of co-sleeping. My position is *against* co-sleeping. However, if you are going to co-sleep, then keep the following points in mind.

- Firm Large Mattress. King size is preferable.
- Water beds, egg-crate mattresses, pillowtop mattresses, and featherbeds are too soft.
- Fitted Sheets need to be tight and flush with the mattress
- Pillows, blankets, quilts, comforters, sheets all should be removed from the sleeping area.
- No stuffed animals
- There should be no gap where the baby can get wedged between the mattress and the headboard, guardrail, or wall. Place a tightly rolled blanket in any possible gaps.
- Sleep positioners are not safe and should not be used.

15

Snoring and Sleep Apnea

Campbell was 2 years old, but you would not think it was a 2 year old girl making the snoring noise that emanated from her room every night. Campbell's parents joked that they had a 2 year old truck driver from the volume of their daughters snoring. She rarely slept through the night, and always looked quite uncomfortable when she did sleep. Campbell would take on odd postures in her princess bed. One leg up, lying horizontally across the mattress, and never would lay the same way for more than 45 minutes. She was not the most happy go lucky

child,frequently waking up "on the wrong side of the crib."
She slept with her mouth open and despite her on an off
sleep through the night, was always on the go during the
day. At her 2 year well child check, Campbell's parents
brought up her worsening behavior and sleep habits to her
pediatrician, who examined her throat and showed the golf
ball sized tonsils to Campbell's parents. "No wonder she
snores" their pediatrician said. Armed with a diagnosis of
likely sleep apnea, they went to a local pediatric Ear Nose
and Throat Surgeon and were recommended to have the
tonsils removed. They proceeded and as early as the day
after the surgery, Campbell snored no more. She finally
looked as if she was getting restful sleep and slept
comfortably. Her behavior and demeanor improved
dramatically, especially in the mornings, where her parents
were amazed and described her as a "new person."

Over the last decade, there is increasing awareness
on the importance of sleep is for toddlers and young
children. Studies actually have shown that 3rd graders
perform at the level of a 1st grader with just one less hour
of sleep per night. The American Academy of Pediatrics
(AAP) recommends that during all physicals, a pediatrician
should at the very least ask about sleeping habits and sleep
problems. If a child snores, then an evaluation to exclude
sleep apnea is the logical next step. Campbell's case is not

uncommon. Sleep apnea is a frequently overlooked cause of behavioral issues and snoring.

How do I know if my child has sleep apnea?

For the purpose of this book, the sleep apnea that we see most frequently (as in Campbell's case) is *Obstructive Sleep Apnea*, in which the tonsils and adenoids (adenoids are essentially tonsils in the back of the nose that you cannot see) get too big and block the normal breathing passage. When your child lies down to sleep, the muscle tone of their throat is more relaxed, and the tonsils fall back onto the throat blocking the air passage more, causing an obstruction, leading to loud snoring. Generally speaking, if your child snores, this is itself is enough to at least bring up to your pediatrician the possibility of sleep apnea. If you child has a nasal quality to his voice, dark circles under his eyes, sleeps in odd positions, is cranky in the morning, snores like a truck driver, and looks like he is struggling to breathe when he is sleeping on his back at night, you need to address the possibility of sleep apnea with your pediatrician.

How do we diagnose Sleep Apnea?

Many cases of sleep apnea due to large tonsils are fairly obvious. Your doctor will look into your child's throat and see huge tonsils. This finding, along with a compatible history of snoring, disturbed sleep, and sleeping in strange positions, is usually enough to make the diagnosis. Sometimes the diagnosis is not so clear cut, and the tonsils are not terribly large, and the history of snoring not as prominent. These subtle cases may need to be investigated further with a procedure called a sleep study. A sleep study is a test performed in a sleep lab, which is a room that looks like a small hotel room, with a bed/crib, video camera, and monitors that determine the oxygen level of the blood, wakefulness and the heartbeat, among other things, as one falls asleep and sleeps through the night. For cases where it is not clear if sleep apnea is a problem, a sleep study is a great tool to help with the diagnosis.

My child was diagnosed with sleep apnea. Now what?

For young children with sleep apnea due to the increased size of the tonsils, the treatment is the removal of the tonsils and usually the adenoids as well (when the tonsils are enlarged, the adenoids are usually also enlarged). The name of the procedure is called a tonsillectomy and adenoidectomy.

Is surgery really necessary for all enlarged tonsils?

No. Enlarged tonsils that are not causing problems can be left alone. However, enlarged tonsils that are obstructing your child's air passage and are effecting the quality of sleep for your child need to be removed.

Is this surgery safe?

A tonsillectomy is one of the most common surgeries performed in children. As with any surgery there are always potential drawbacks to the procedure, such as infection, bleeding complications, not enough of the tonsil being removed, risk of anesthesia, requiring a second operation down the road, and dysfunction of the voice and palate requiring speech therapy. The decision to undergo an operation for a child should be taken seriously. However, if your child has obstructive sleep apnea, the risks of the surgery are usually outweighed by the potential benefits of curing the sleep apnea. You should always have an opportunity to discuss the risks and benefits with your pediatrician and your surgeon. The surgery usually takes about 15-30 minutes. Depending on the degree of sleep apnea and the age, some children may have to spend the night after the surgery, which many may go home several hours after the surgery. I always recommend to parents that you ask your Ear Nose and Throat (ENT) surgeon how many of these procedures they have done. You should only have your child's surgery performed by a surgeon that has performed thousands.

Conclusion

I hope the information presented in this text helped you gain knowledge about the cause of your child's sleep problems, and how to approach your baby's sleep challenges. Be consistent, loving, and patient as you implement the techniques presented here and you will be rewarded with a happy, healthy baby that sleeps, *like a baby*.

Made in the USA
San Bernardino, CA
07 January 2014